5
by
Five

5 by Five

Five Poems by Five Poets

Danielle Bizzarro
Jeff Carroll
Andrea Denny-Brown
Sarah Hannah
Robert Pestka

A Wit's End Imprint

National Library of Canada Cataloguing in Publication Data

Main entry under title:

5 by five

ISBN 1-55212-679-X

1. American poetry--21st century.   I. Pestka, Robert, 1966-   II.
Title: Five by five.
PS615.F53 2001   811'.608   C2001-910459-6

TRAFFORD

This book was published *on-demand* in cooperation with Trafford Publishing.
On-demand publishing is a unique process and service of making a book available for retail sale to the public taking advantage of on-demand manufacturing and Internet marketing.
On-demand publishing includes promotions, retail sales, manufacturing, order fulfilment, accounting and collecting royalties on behalf of the author.

Suite 6E, 2333 Government St., Victoria, B.C. V8T 4P4, CANADA

Phone	250-383-6864	Toll-free	1-888-232-4444 (Canada & US)
Fax	250-383-6804	E-mail	sales@trafford.com
Web site	www.trafford.com	TRAFFORD PUBLISHING IS A DIVISION OF TRAFFORD HOLDINGS LTD.
Trafford Catalogue #01-0078		www.trafford.com/robots/01-0078.html	

10   9   8   7   6   5   4   3

—For those who taught us the value
of the written word.

Contents

I.

II.

5 by Five

I.

Danielle

Shelter Island

Monday dawn
before the rush hour crowds
the dock, the hard edge of the moon lingers
high in the rising light.

The first boat back ferries the odds
and ends of the long weekend
and of the season—
the reading lamp and fancy chair
battened down but out of context
on board without people.
Stand back please, so we can leave
he winks then grins.
And we slip away easily.
Morning drifts along the beach.

Out on the Sound, as the sun
floods a cut of road afloat
I should relax but still harbor
the silly dread of leaving
the iron on, the milk out in the kitchen
the small living thing mistakenly
locked away in the shifting shades
of the boughed house.

As we coast in
the weighted dock heaves then lists.
And road engages road again.
Stand back, please
as I prepare to leave
against the tide
of newspapers and wristwatches.

Andrea

Backward

from the brown lizard-shaped stain
on the front of her white dress
to the chemicals he told her are secreted
from a gland in the lower lip so when
they kiss they become addicted
to one another's saliva like nicotine
he said like cocaine she said
and with her tongue explored that tiny ridge
below the pudgy worm-flesh inside his lip
and thought this chemical thing is a real possibility
but she's not thinking straight anymore
she's working back to the night before
when laughing he told her he'd lied
he isn't single after all and she took it
in a breath 'cause she was hooked already
sleeves rolled past her elbows
no jacket because the day was hot
not like the day before damp and dark
when they returned from their long walk
re-entered the party from the side door
one guilty fork between them
as they shared the last piece of cake
and the walk itself an echo
of the smooth stones they'd slung
from the beach at the base of the cliff they'd skidded
down on their heels as they talked
about beach erosion after he kissed her
just out of sight of the house ten feet
past the vineyard when the inch
of red wine in her glass had splashed
past the crystal lip through the air and up
onto the dry cotton lap of her dress and hung there
brilliant and crimson in the gusty wind.

Robert

A Dam on the Euphrates

where the Romans
and Parthians
met

pistachio trees grow
in hills
rising

from the river
a settlement
founded

by Alexander's general
in 250
B.C.

Seleucia and Apamea
two towns
joined

by a bridge
the only
crossing-point

from the Taurus
Mountains to
Babylonia

Greek, Roman, Aramaic,
Iranian and
Mesopotamian

cultures mingled in
this city
burned

by Sassanids in
250 A.D.
buried

for two millennia
hidden from
archaeologists

frantic to rescue
sui generis
treasures

before the rising
waters engulf
ruins

of the ancient
bridge crossing
Zeugma

Andrea

Calamity's Sonnet

There is a hairdresser in Grozny, Chechnya,
Who sets up shop on a broken street, where
Vacant windows gape at her petunia-
Scented oil, hand-creams, combs for long hair.
Each customer has something buried to tell:
That man carries his dead son in his eyes,
This woman cowered as thundering shells
Shattered her home. Here she is going to dye
Her hair blonde, it's the new look of the old
Country. With oiled elbows, scented wrists
She will walk the torn city like a shiny needle,
Try to sew each gash with a clean stitch.
I know. At your funeral I wore *Drumbeat Red*
On my lips for you, but you were still dead.

Jeff

Alpha Bar Omega

A cold iron is raised over the rail of the corral.
On its dark head is carved an immovable grimace through which
shines the winter sky. A small boy, bundled in coat and hat,

sits on a stump watching while his father
takes hold of the long, stiff rod, holding it in his left hand
while he rakes coals at the base of a fire, then buries the dark head

into embers. The boy is too young to know what day it is,
what month, what season. He notices his breath.
The hoof-pocked mud of the corral, glistening

and crunching in the frosted morning, appeals. A gate opens.
More men enter the corral leading the first calf. They throw the calf
down onto its side. One man kneels, straddling the calf's throat.

Another ropes the ankles, and they all pull the line,
drawing the hooves tightly together. The father begins in the fire
to stir coals. He raises the rod. Smoke peels away from the iron,

the face of it glowing red, no longer bearing a grimace but grinning
ghastly as it kisses calf-flesh. Searing hiss. The calf struggles.
Smokesteam rises around the father's forearms. The calf, shaken,

unharmed, is unbound. It bolts through the gate into the pasture,
leaping, twisting, craning its neck around toward the new mark, toward
the morpheme, toward the language that it would find useless until it was lost.

Danielle

Al Fresco

Last seen in these Venetian streets, a girl
Leaning by a remote fountain. Lost within
The flaming swirls of her painted skirts,
In cool echoes of the past, she begins

Her parting letter, now thrown in sharp relief
By such a brilliant shade of sea, all seems
Brief and real beneath her. Gold leaf.
You hope to steal her from the prior dreamer.

Chiaroscuro. Are you sure she's no more
Than a shadow cast by a bridge of sighs
In the twilight of your day's desire?
If but a figment left riding with the tides,

As evening breezes in its private longing,
You might consider the more subtle hues
Under which she's most obliged to linger:
Your nighttime sky or this forever blue.

Sarah

You Are Perseus, but I Am Not Andromeda

To begin, I'm pale but not that pretty,
Tied and sad at times, but not completely
Helpless, although my circumstance alarms;
Parents mill about, waving their arms.
You know you could win them over; you dove
Down and won me. Half-drowning I was reedy:
A clutch of swaying tendrils in the sea.
I was softened in that silty cove,
Blindly feeding, green and pliable.
Then I rose for air, and there, like coral,
I changed my disposition. I'm the muse
But not the maiden—yours, but not the prize,
Fresh and chaste and dowried, you think you're due.
I'm the jagged rock you cling to.

Robert

Overlooking the River at Orléans
for Charles

I fit you into this picture
As I have into a hundred before.
You are the pilot of a drifting barge,
A passing cyclist, or a bird—
Always *le coup de pouce.*

I have sat alone like this engaged
In conversation—
                    you favored
Chalk-speckled earth to my field of blue sky
The river curling toward a constant horizon
Cypress high above riverbank willows.

Today the church towers will be hidden.
The farmers will work deliberately, the plums
Will be blue, this once-sieged city now
A valley of fruits and vegetables, the fog
Revealing overripe grapes on the river's slope.

That your gouache form
Is carried away in some distant current
Will not keep your image
From growing stronger.

le coup de pouce: final touch, final stroke

Jeff

On Living Alone In A Wintry Place

Early evenings and cold late nights
in a boarding house in January, sometimes not alone
but with a bottle of wine, a book, a meal,
and a candle; snow thick on the roof. Often,
the sounds of the madman living below wheezing
in and out of dementia and of the girl who only needed
a place to sleep.

Long walks at night in the cold to the graveyard
at the top of the hill, watching the tail of a dog
trail off in the moonlight through the trees—
the terrible way the snow becomes dark out there,
like memory. The dreadful way in which
we are drawn into it. Believing we can
turn away from it. Believing we want to.

Danielle

On the Laws of Motion

My beautiful, sly, little, grown-up boy,
Although I ought to, how do I eschew
Rugged leather for mended corduroy
When, choosing so, I'm bound to lose you?
It's sound advice from friends who tend to tire
Quickly of life and liability;
Nice, if a quiet idle drives you wild,
If you'd skirt passion for civility.
With regret, all moving bodies must come
To rest—friction's consequence. Why deny
It? We might turn instead onto the highway
And ride, trailing sparks behind for untold
Miles, despite the wind smacking the Harley—
Rattled a bit, perhaps, but hardly sorry.

Robert

Saturday Night
for K---

I.
I had reserved
this evening
for my darling
you. Then
at the last minute—

Here I am
crouched in the corner
looking at everything
suspiciously.
The cat fades in
and drops
a quivering mouse
on my feet. I eat
it. So what.

When you emerge
from self-reflection
will you have
psyched *me*
into oblivion?

II.
I had reserved
this evening
for my darling
you. At last
pen is in hand.

There is this
weight
of metaphor
this lightness of
irony this
semantic exactitude
bearing down on me.
I stumble
and am hurled
off the edge
of the world.

Do I need suffering
to realize
these words?

III.
I have seen
passion
so perfectly fitting
that it wears
no clothes.

Imagine this: a poem
so telling
you recall
exactly
what it's like
to kiss me on the lips.

This anxiety
is a pair of long
black gloves;
your fingers,
like these lines—
such great
expectations.

Sarah

Snow Drift

I only want to write about a space
Three-inches square, in the picket fence's
Stolid corner, that uncontested crevice
Boasting, suddenly, a jagged occurrence
Of snow, Alp-like, resting on the brief ledge
The wooden crossbeam makes: unlikely cliff,
However wedged, suggesting passage
Beyond lawn and property line, as if
Transgression could be intimately known
Through bold example in miniature,
On familiar ground, a trace of snow blown
On a fence, articulation of a dare:
To realize the route the mountain sees,
The fall to nether—valley, wild trees.

II.

Robert

The City In Which Your Granddaughter Lives
for Mie Suzuki

1. The streets are empty—
   each window holds a buzzing
   air conditioner.

2. In the park a dog
   stirs up dry leaves—which settle
   slowly to the ground.

3. A wet cigarette
   on his lip—the man to whom
   I offer steamed rice.

4. Skyscrapers reflect
   a row of pearl-blossom trees—
   muted in dark glass.

Sarah

The Colors Are Off This Season

I want none of this solemn pall—
These orange fireside hues,
Fading sun, autumnal tumble,
Stricken, inimitable—Rose.

I want Pink, unthinking, true.
Foam pink, cream and coddle,
Miniskirt, Lolita, pompom, tutu,
Milkshake. Pink without the mottle

Or the dying fall. Pink adored, a thrall
So pale it's practically white.
A tinted room beneath a gable—
Ice pink, powder, feather-light—

Untried corner of the treble.
I want the lift, not the lower.
Bloodless pink stalled at girl,
No weight, no care, no hour.

Andrea

Black Leather Pants

Low riding, button-up,
hand-sewn black leather,
back pockets only, with
a slight flair at the ankle.
I think about them lately,
watching the teenage girls
on the subway flaunt their
well-worn bell-bottoms,
dragging with indignant
pride on the filthly ground
around their sneakers.
Yours weren't like that.
Hand-tailored in London
to fit your ass exactly,
to lengthen your legs
and accent platform shoes;
you roamed the streets
of Europe in these pants
in the early 70's, young
and sexy, in and out of clubs
with other younger, sexier men.
By the time I met you
you were an established
smart-ass in Boston's South End.
You called me *bitch-slut-whore*
in your flawless Zimbabwean accent
and I didn't mind, it was just
the lingo behind the scenes.

You made the costumes that I wore,
a fresh hire at the back of the ballet;
you favored me, on your better days,
though I never understood why.
I was young and shy,
and in the days before you died
you pulled out these black leather pants,
ordered me to try them on,
and with one dramatic glance around
(no family, no lost romance)
said *they* deserved a second chance.

Robert

Still Life

I.   when it finally happened
        that I gave him that token
        my idea of him had withered
                from a fat
                blue
                plum

        when after many years
        I touched her and meant it
        her thoughts had wandered
                behind a wall
                of prickly pear

        when I felt it
        I dared not tell it or
        like a cherry tree
                risk
                losing
                blossom

II.   a photograph of fruit
in a coarse wooden bowl
fiery skins of peaches
            break
            panes
            of patterned light

tear up old photos
unblemished fruit set
on silver salt emulsion
            falls to pieces
            in your hand

take up a mottled fig
and as it ripens
press its swollen flesh
            to your
            quivering
            tongue

Sarah

Lethe

I've hit bottom now—your murky water.
Too breathless to swim, too freighted to float,
I sank from light and shore, my dress wrapped strait
Around my limbs, preventing any stir.
And this is how you thrive, consummate host,
Coaxing reeds from your edges, roots from soil,
Now sparkling in conquest, now misted and still,
But not inert, planning tributary, tryst.
There must be a way out (not how I came),
But if I knew, I forgot in the lace
Of your currents, in the deep chills that numb,
In your muddy lips' promise: *Drink. No Blame.*
What sweet obliterations bloom in a kiss—
Morphines, poppies, plums.

Jeff

Index of Refraction

I begin to recall a boy who carried once
a moon-shaped stone out onto a bridge.
When he got half way across he turned.
He hefted the stoneheavy object over the rail and
had he not let go of it the boy too would have gone on over.
Nor had he thought that there might be someone beneath
the bridge, a fisherman say, in a boat, sounding the river
with a line, perhaps fishing for trout or majestic steelhead
running the cold green depths.

There was not such a man. Though that was not
for the boy's sake. It was merely a fortunate lack
of coincidence. There was only the river swallowing
the stone with a quick noise, the stone dropping first
through one, and then more slowly through another
atmosphere, resting finally obscured in the deep
slimebottom of the river. The boy had not altered
its course, but the river, however slightly,
was altered. I turn from the window and walk back

to where my wife lies sleeping. The left side of her face
is basked in moonlight, the right in darkness. I had locked
the doors earlier, and I remember having double-checked
those locks, but I see that it has crept in anyway. I move
quickly to my daughter's room, hoping to get there in time.
I want to warn her. But when I get there, standing over her, I see
that her entire face shines with moonlight. I forget what I wanted
to warn her about. I stand for I don't know how long.
When finally I turn to leave I am already wondering
what bridge? How long ago?

Danielle

While You Were Out

I dropped
       by to borrow
back the better part
       of an hour I'd left you
long ago and hope
       you don't mind. It was all
very spontaneous, the stars
       overhead, the call
on the phone, your answering
       machine cutting me
off before I was
       through, the moon in
then out of focus, tangled
       in your hair. I must have been
out of my mind. I jimmied
       your lock only to knock
over a pot of petunias,
       to leave—the only evidence
of this first offense, the tiny pile of time
       that I dared not bury
with my bare hands.

Andrea

Familiars

I dream that cats come to me at night.
Black birds, a sheep with three horns curling
and a smell I like, a snake or two,
a dog with one pale blue eye, one brown.
They come to tell me they have made it
through the wilderness. They tell me they are hungry
and beneath my rib a teat appears.
They suckle and spit, drink their fill. They lie
on their backs, round bellies shining in the moonlight
like mushroom tops. I am gardening,
I must get the crop in before the frost.
I pluck ears of corn and carry them
in the fold of my skirt until I can carry no more.
I ask the animals where they came from,
where they are going. And they call me cunning.
My full skirt becomes my belly, I am pregnant.
One by one they kiss my hand when they leave,
and I know somehow I've been betrayed.

Jeff

Friday Night

Deep in Thought,
Indiana
where Salvatore Quasimodo
still rings in the
ears, my footsteps are variable tonight.
From my mouth flow silver breathclouds in the moonlight.
I reach down into the grave
and pull myself, by the ankles, out.

My body is naked and smeared with mud,
only partly decomposed.
I lie down beside myself, appearing
neon tetra before the crowd which
orders me to stand and walk.
I stand. I walk, walking unholy waters, speaking
unholy tongues, working unholy
miracles. I am neither in heaven

n/or out of heaven. Neither chambered
n/or antechambered. Neither membered
n/or remembered. Searching for words
I find my loins. I raise my loins, condense my
loins, stretch out my loins. Speak my loins.
Holding my loins I say,
"These are my loins!
I'm embedded in my loins!"

Danielle

Vandals

In a dented shack
back in the woods
behind the old man's house
we rummaged through rusted tools
paint cans, screws, old shoes and other junk
left to rot.
You pocketed a copper hinge and dropped
on the damp stacks of *Life* still tied
tight in manageable bundles while I
pried the lock on a dusty tin box.
We cleared a corner.

Then something brushed
up against me briefly
in the dark
just as I caught that glimpse of you
in the last bit of light
streaming through
a long tear in the roof—
your hands, much cooler than
the hard dirt beneath me.

At dusk, roused
by the neighbor's hounds
we stumbled out laughing
then planted a handful
of the seed we'd scattered
just to see
before we soaked the pile of papers and rags and—
almost as an afterthought—
lit the match and ran.

Andrea

Saved

Later I lie in bed,
picturing myself
in the same situation,
glancing around
the apartment at all my things:
My ragged *Aeneid*,
our niece's stick figure
paintings on the fridge:
a blue you, hand
in hand with an orange,
red-mouthed me.
What to single out?
Your grandmother's ring,
the one you gave me
for my thirtieth birthday,
the night we escaped
July's heat by sitting
waist-deep in the cool bath,
drinking salty margaritas
and discussing the teen
angst of our unborn children?
I imagine the barely-opened
wedding gifts stowed
under the bed, the letters
we sent that year
we lived apart, inflamed
and curling into themselves.

I think briefly of the cream
Versace dress bought on sale
but never worn, the one
that slips proudly over my hips
and refuses all attempts
at demureness. Would I leave
it all behind to burn
with the dust balls
and the roach traps, join
you and the cat waiting
safely on the street;
or would I stand frozen
in indecision,
rapt and silent,
fire hissing whispers
in my hair?

Jeff

Mephiticus

There was a horizon once
gray-drawn against the dark.
It has become a nighthouse;
soiled brick. Something is
unstable. There is a random issue

on the path to the door. The yard
is flooded, stenched and stagnant.
The goat is dead.
It floats bloated on its bellyside.
I want to know who is
responsible. Who is there here

who can stand it? Give account.
You. You there, emerging,
holding something. Holding it fully, I see.
Is that responsibility? I'd say you're full
in the thicket and slopping over.
I'd say you're guilty. Are you ashamed?

If you are not ashamed then come, follow
me. Follow me through here. We'll track back
where I've already slogged through the undertent.
Let me smell your fingers. Are they as mine?
Do they smell of blood rot? Look!
Just up ahead. It is exactly late summer.
Look! Wildflowers.
Coleus.
Up ahead.

Sarah

Lunar Landing

The foot set down:
A work-in-progress

On a dry surface,
A text of treads bowed

Slightly by the human arch,
Toe shadowed. The sense

Cannot be reckoned—
Between where you are

And where you were—
The avoirdupois difference

Between the emblem
And the thing that made it,

The extension
Of a body in a state

Of compromised magnetics:
Disencumbered,

Skipping on granules, in sun—
Another angle altogether.

ISBN 155212679-X

9 781552 126790